Crazy
Chewing Gum

by Wendy Blaxland
illustrated by Jan D'Silva

Harcourt Achieve

Rigby • Saxon • Steck-Vaughn

www.HarcourtAchieve.com
1.800.531.5015

Characters

Declan

Mom

Foggy

Contents

Chapter 1

A Recipe for Trouble

Mom hates chewing gum. She won't have it in the house.

"Gum is nasty stuff," she says. "It gets *everywhere!*"

So I want to make my own. I look on the Internet for recipes.

Super Strawberry sounds good.

I shut my door and mix.

I'm just adding the glowing pink food coloring when Mom knocks on the door.

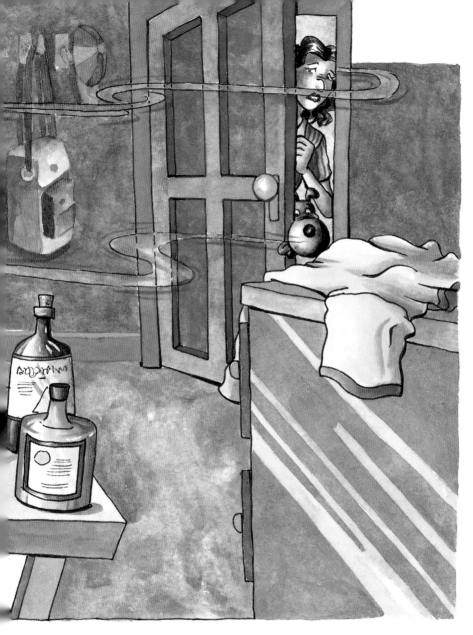

"Declan, what's that smell?" she asks.
"Are you experimenting again?"

"Don't come in," I call, sweeping it all into my drawer. "It's a surprise."

Foggy pushes the door open. She shoves her nose into the drawer.

One of the powders tips into my strawberry mixture.

Chapter 2

Problem Pets

"Out of there!" I yell.

I pull Foggy's head out. A bright pink ribbon flies out, too.

The gum is stuck to her nose. Her nose is a bright glowing pink!

Mom goes ballistic.

"Declan!" she shouts.

Foggy tries to wipe the chewing gum off.

Now Foggy has pink stuff on her nose
and her paw.

"Hold still, Foggy," I say as Misty, the
cat, walks in.

Misty takes a swipe at the long loop
of pink chewing gum.

She wipes it on the carpet. Then she
wipes it on her whiskers.

"What is it?" cries Mom.

"Um . . . it's . . . um . . . special, super gum-glue," I say. "Smells like gum, acts like glue."

Chapter 3

A Glowing Family

"Super mess is more like it," says Mom.

"I'm home," Dad says, walking into
my room.

Foggy runs and jumps on Dad. Bright
pink strings hang from his jacket.

"Hey, this is my good suit," says Dad, wiping it off. The pink strings stick to his hands.

"For goodness sake, Declan," he says as my sister Susie walks in.

"What's all the pink stuff?" Susie asks as she scoops up Misty. She looks down.

"My new top!" she cries.

"Nobody move," Mom orders. "Now Declan, what is this gum-glue?"

"Chewing gum, Mom," I admit. I pull out
a lump and pop it in my mouth.
Big mistake!

"Go on," says Dad.

I shake my head. This gum-glue is super sticky.

My teeth are stuck together. I can only gurgle.

"Right," says Dad. "We need to get some help."

Chapter 4

Hard Work

They decide to take the animals to the vet first.

"Her fur will grow back soon," the vet says.

"As for Foggy's pink nose, maybe it'll wear off," says the vet.

"I've never seen anything like it."

25

Next we go to the dentist. His drill
overheats. He adds the cost of the
drill to our bill.

It'll take me months to pay everyone back. I have to wash the car all year to pay for Dad's new suit.

Mom says I will have to live with my pink-spotted carpet.

Unless I invent something to clean it off!

What about homemade cotton candy?
Don't you think it should come in
different colors? Let's just switch on
the computer . . .

Glossary

admit
own up, tell the truth

ballistic
very, very angry

drill
a tool to make holes

experimenting
testing

gurgle
to make a bubbling noise

invent
to make something

muttered
said quietly

overheats
stops working because
it's too hot

swipe
a quick arm movement

Wendy Blaxland

Chewing gum is amazing stuff. Once, my toddler son sat down outside on some very sticky pink chewing gum. When I warned him that he might have sat in gum, he got up and kept turning around to try to see his bottom. Soon a long thread of sticky pink chewing gum wound itself around everyone who tried to help. At least it made us all laugh!

Jan D'Silva

He thought he could blow the world's biggest bubble...

but....